GETT

LAN(

Beryl Dixon

TROTMAN

This first edition published in 1995
by Trotman and Company Ltd
12 Hill Rise, Richmond, Surrey TW10 6UA

© Trotman and Company Limited 1995

British Library Cataloguing in Publication Data
A catalogue record for this book is available from the
British Library.

ISBN 0 85660 169 1

Printed and bound in Great Britain

CONTENTS

ABOUT THE AUTHOR

Beryl Dixon is a freelance careers and education writer, and a part-time careers and higher education adviser at a tertiary college. She is a regular contributor to *The Times* and author of numerous books and articles.

Chapter One
CAREERS USING LANGUAGES

The fact that you have picked up this book probably means that you are hoping to use languages in your career. You will be able to do so. The British seem finally to be overcoming their reluctance to learn other people's languages. We have realised that, even though English remains the universal language, there are advantages to communicating with people from other countries in their language rather than expecting all the world to learn ours. The ability to speak and understand other languages is vital for communicating, for negotiating – in careers as diverse as sales and marketing, international finance and banking, tourism and in the diplomatic service.

But – and it is a big but – it is that phrase 'use languages *in* your career' that is important. There is a big distinction between using languages as an additional skill in a job and earning a living through the use of languages alone. A very small proportion of all the students who have taken languages degrees work as professional linguists. For most, languages must be seen as *a secondary skill*.

The big three careers which do primarily make use of languages are:

• translating
• interpreting
• teaching.

We will look at these first, then go on to examine other careers which can be entered by people with qualifications in languages *provided that they are willing to acquire further qualifications or to pick up the necessary skills* once in employment.

☐ TRANSLATING

Translators work with the written word. They may translate anything from letters and reports to books, articles, technical and scientific publications. What many people do not realise is that professional translators work into their mother tongue. Indeed, the Institute of Translation and Interpreting offers this advice to would-be translators: 'Don't offer to translate into languages other than your mother tongue as this will mark you as an amateur.' Consequently, if you hope to become a translator, you should have an excellent command of written English. This is as important as a good knowledge of foreign languages. It must be stressed that demand for translators is small. To have any chance at all of earning a living through translating you should have an excellent knowledge of at least two languages other than your own. Keyboard skills are almost obligatory. Although some people may get away with using a dictating machine this means that an employer has to pay two people – the translator and the typist who subsequently types up the translation and who also needs a reasonable knowledge of the language being used in order to avoid raising too many queries. You should also have the kind of mind that enjoys wrestling with a phrase in order to get it just right – technically correct without losing the flavour of the original. It helps too, if you can offer knowledge of specialised subjects, such as law, transport, commerce or current affairs in which you are up to date with current vocabulary and jargon.

Most professional translators in full-time employment have a postgraduate diploma in translating in addition to their first degree in languages. This is not absolutely essential – especially if the languages degree has included translation techniques. The fact remains, though, that translating is a skill which has to be learned like any other. Add to that the competitive nature of the career and you understand why most top translators do have a specialist diploma.

Where do translators work?

Staff translators, that is those in full-time employment, work for large companies, research organisations, government departments and international organisations. The European Commission in Brussels is a major employer of translators, since documents have to be translated from and into every one of the European Union's languages.

Freelance translators work from their own homes, accepting work from all kinds of clients on a fee-paying basis. It can be difficult to become established as a freelance translator without having plentiful contacts as sources of work. Many people start freelance translating as a side-line while in other employment, perhaps in teaching or in a staff translator's position, then become totally self-employed as their reputation grows and work builds up. If this line of work attracted you, you would need the ability to market your service and the self-discipline to make yourself work every day with no boss standing over you. You would also have to invest in some equipment, notably a word processor or PC with software capable of handling foreign accents, dictionaries, an answerphone and a fax.

☐ INTERPRETING

If there are limited openings for translators there are even fewer for interpreters! Interpreters use the spoken language and, unlike translators, may translate to and from several languages. There are two kinds of interpreting:

- Simultaneous interpreting involves the interpreter in oral translation into another language about half a sentence behind the speaker. In conference interpreting, the interpreter normally sits in a booth and translates as the speaker at the front delivers an address. This is relayed to other delegates via headphones.

- Consecutive interpreting means that the interpreter takes notes of what is being said (usually in a fairly small or even one-to-one meeting) and relays the speakers' words to each other every few minutes.

- Liaison interpreting is a combination of both methods and involves the interpreter in translating from both languages while two people are speaking to each other. This kind of interpreting is done, for example, when two heads of state meet. The anonymous person you see standing right behind them in news bulletins is usually not the bodyguard but the interpreter.

In addition to excellent language skills, interpreters need stamina and powers of concentration. There is a story of one whose attention wandered during a Brussels agricultural conference and who then rendered 'frozen semen' as 'frozen sailor' (seaman). Most interpreters have their own anecdotes of similar howlers.

Interpreters vary in their views as to which of the two forms of interpreting is the more stressful. Some say that consecutive work is very demanding. Listening to Japanese for 15 minutes, then speaking in English for 15 minutes more can be tiring. However, simultaneous interpreting is widely regarded as exhausting. In fact, interpreters rarely work for more than 30 minutes without a break from the microphone.

Where do interpreters work?

There are *some* staff jobs for interpreters, mainly at the European Commission (the largest employer), the UN and similar organisations, but even these employ large numbers of freelance interpreters as required. Most of the work is actually freelance.

A less well-known but growing field of interpreting work is community interpreting which is translating for the courts, police, immigration officials and sometimes for doctors.

Even including freelance work, there are very few openings for interpreters anywhere in the world. The Association Internationale des Interprètes de Conference (AIIC), the conference interpreters' professional body, has only 2,000 members worldwide. Not all interpreters choose to join this association, of course.

Many British interpreters are members of the Institute of Translation and Interpreting (ITI).

It is pretty rare to earn a living by interpreting alone. Most interpreters, including some AIIC members, do additional work, combining interpreting with teaching, lecturing or translating.

☐ TEACHING

We all know something about this. French is still the most commonly taught language in British secondary schools, followed by German, but there are some areas where Spanish is now taught as the first foreign language. Russian and Italian feature on some schools' timetables as do minority languages. However, if you want to teach, you should equip yourself with one commonly taught one and, in order to have a good choice of jobs, you should be able to teach two. It goes without saying that you should enjoy teaching! You won't survive long if you love languages but hate pupils.

Teachers are employed in secondary schools and further education colleges and in universities and institutes of higher education (where they are known as lecturers). There are good opportunities for additional work at evening centres or for part-time work in both evening and day-time classes in the adult education sector.

Teaching English as a foreign language is something which attracts a lot of people. It is often known by its initials - TEFL or simply EFL. It is not necessary to have a degree or any qualification in languages to become an EFL teacher, since most such teaching is done by the 'direct' method, using English only in classes. However, having learned foreign languages yourself is a great help when working in TEFL. You have more understanding of the pupils' needs, of the difficulties they are encountering, and if you happen to understand their language you usually know why they are making certain mistakes – often because they are using constructions directly translated from their own language. For example, at a very simple level if you know how to say 'I'm hot' in French, you will realise why French pupils translating literally from their own language might say that they have heat. You would know why they were saying that something had pleased them rather than that they liked it.

There are opportunities to work in language schools in this country but far more overseas, particularly in Europe and the Middle East. The chance to spend some years in a foreign country is what attracts many people to TEFL.

Two other forms of English language teaching are English as a Second Language (ESL) and English for Specific Purposes (ESP). ESL work is mainly with immigrants to Britain or to other English speaking countries who need to learn English to a high level or in countries which use English as the official language of communication, such as, some Comonwealth countries. ESP is really only suitable for teachers with some kind of scientific or technical knowledge since it usually involves teaching the language to engineers, business people or scientists.

There is yet a third set of initials! EAP or English for Academic Purposes refers to tuition for international students who intend to take a higher education course in Britain. They usually come in advance of their course to bring their English up to the level needed to study in higher education and to acquire some specialised vocabulary.

In order to teach in state schools in Britain, you would have to take a one-year courseof training known as a Postgraduate Certificate in Education (PGCE), during which you would learn how to teach your subject and do some teaching practice in schools. The PGCE has the advantage of being the one postgraduate course for which students automatically receive a grant. Currently there is such a shortage of modern languages teachers that students on this course also receive an additional sum of money known as a bursary.

TEFL teachers can train by taking courses of almost any length. These are offered by various organisations (and can be quite expensive). In order to have a choice of job and of employer (especially of employers who offer decent contracts and working conditions, since some language schools give very poor rates of pay), it is advisable to take a course which leads to the Royal Society of Arts (RSA)/Cambridge qualification. This is recognised and respected all over the world. Short courses are run by commercial organisations – but the qualification may lead only to employment in one of that organisation's schools. Some PGCE courses concentrate on TESL.

OTHER CAREERS

Careers in which languages are very important include:

☐ BI-LINGUAL SECRETARIAL WORK

Secretaries or personal assistants (PAs), as the top ones tend to be called, are assistants to managers. They do a great deal of administration and are often in charge of running an office which may have one or two junior employees in it. They are also the experts in office technology and equipment. Frequently their bosses expect them to decide which word processor or computer to use – and to purchase it. They organise conferences, make travel arangements and often are responsible for deciding which travel companies and hotels their managers use.

Many have their own junior assistant who does most of the routine work.

Secretaries who are also qualified in languages do their normal secretarial duties plus as much language work as is required by their employer. This varies considerably from simply typing the occasional letter in a foreign language to translating much of the correspondence that comes in, translating letters dictated in English into another language and typing them, using the phone frequently, meeting and looking after foreign visitors, reading foreign newspapers and magazines and making summaries of important articles. Since the language content of a job can vary so much, secretaries have to check the job description very carefully or change employers until they find the right combination of duties.

Even highly paid PAs, however, still do some typing and many senior executives still expect shorthand, even though audio typing has made a big impact. Employers are also very interested in typing and shorthand speeds. Foreign shorthand is not always required but can help to get the right job. It is important to do a *good* course – one that teaches all the skills and at a college that has a good reputation for guiding its leavers into the right kind of employment.

Where do bi-lingual secretaries/PAs work?

Work is available in this country with British companies that do overseas trade, with *foreign* companies that have opened regional offices in the UK, with international and multinational organisations, with legal and financial institutions and in government departments, particularly the Foreign Office, and the Department of Trade and Industry.

There are also many opportunities to live and work in other countries, particularly if you have learned foreign shorthand. There are jobs in most European Union countries, with companies and at the European institutions themselves in Brussels, Luxembourg and Strasbourg. If you are independent, mature and prepared to adjust to a different culture you might enjoy working for a foreign employer. In this case you would be employed mainly for your knowledge of *English*. You would probably find yourself translating documents into English, correcting correspondence and handling telephone calls to the UK. Your foreign language would be the one in which you worked – and, of course, you would need it for daily living.

Which languages should a secretary speak? See Chapter Two but also bear in mind that almost any language will be required by some employer somewhere. Leading London recruitment agencies which place secretaries in all kinds of companies are currently finding some demand for Russian (a few years ago only a handful of companies traded with Russia, compared with hundreds today), plus less usual languages such as Hungarian, Portuguese (spoken in Brazil as well as in Portugal itself), Japanese and Arabic. That is in addition to continuing demand for the more common ones.

☐ GOVERNMENT SERVICE

The Government is a major employer of linguists. Linguist specialists, as they are called, work in Cheltenham at the Joint Technical Language Service. The work is covered by the Official Secrets Act which makes it difficult to find out in advance very much about the nature of the work involved and means that once you are in, you cannot talk about your work to anyone else! It is pure language work, however, and involves translating, transcribing and researching into languages. Interpreters and translators are employed by the Ministry of Defence, again on work of a secret nature, and translators are employed in a few other government departments in central London.

The Diplomatic Service is a firm favourite with language graduates and like any other popular employer, can be highly selective. It isn't necessary to have any knowledge of languages, although most applicants do. They will teach you any you are required to learn. A spokesperson says that only if two applicants are neck and neck for a position, equally suitable in every way, but one speaks one or more foreign languages, may linguistic ability be the deciding factor.

Diplomats spend up to two-thirds of their working lives abroad. They are expected to accept any posting (and these are changed every two or three years) and to serve where they are needed. Personal preference is taken into account where possible and the Service is now trying to post couples to the same country. It has even brought in the facility for either partner to take a period of unpaid leave if no suitable joint posting can be found and return to work after a gap with no loss of seniority.

What do Diplomatic Service staff do?

Basically, they represent Britain in other countries and look after the interests of British nationals working overseas. They staff embassies and consulates, promote British interests, try to ease the way for British companies hoping to do business in a new market and stay in touch with the expatriate British community, ready to act in the case of any national emergency or hostile situation (which could involve advising people to leave the country and organising the evacuation). They also deal with requests from people of other nationalities wishing to come here.

It is quite common to retrain in new languages in Government Service, particularly in the so-called 'hard' languages like Arabic, Chinese or Persian. Training is provided and is excellent. Indeed, you may never use the language of your degree in your entire career!

☐ THE EUROPEAN INSTITUTIONS

There are openings for most of the same kinds of work that are available in British Government Service in the European institutions (Parliament, the Commission, the Council and the courts). Several thousand administrators are employed in the three major cities of Brussels, Luxembourg and Strasbourg. If you like the sound of becoming a Eurocrat it's worth knowing that Britain is still somewhat under-represented. We don't apply for the vacant positions in anything like the same numbers as the French do for example. One problem has been in the past that people simply didn't know when jobs were likely to come up. (They are always advertised in the national press). The Government is endeavouring to do something about recruitment at the highest levels through its introduction of a 'fast stream' entry to the Home Civil Service which is particularly geared to getting staff to apply for the EU jobs as they arise - and coaching them in techniques for passing the selection tests.

☐ SALES AND MARKETING

'When I come to sell to you in England then I will speak English, but when you come to sell to me in Germany *dann müssen Sie Deutsch sprechen!*', said Willy Brandt. In other words, if you are trying to persuade someone to buy something from you the ball is in their court. They decide whether or not to be impressed by your sales pitch. It is up to you to convince them by your presentation. How much more likely it is that you will do so by speaking the customer's language.

Marketing is defined by the Institute of Marketing as 'supplying the right goods at the right price at the right time'. A marketing department within a company carries out research to identify a need for a product and/or to establish individual customer's requirements, coordinates pricing, packaging and advertising. Most large firms and recruit a number of graduates each year as management trainees. Those that are involved in export marketing – that is promoting products in other countries – are interested in trainees who can speak or who can learn languages. If you are fluent in two languages and the company does business in a country whose language you don't speak, it doesn't matter. You have linguistic ability. They can and will send you on an intensive course designed especially for business executives. (See Chapter Six).

Languages alone will not get you a job in marketing, however. You will be in competition with graduates in other subjects, perhaps from business studies courses, who can also attend intensive language courses. But if you have the right personality and the skills the employer demands, you will have the edge.

Why? Because you have proven linguistic ability. You will also have some appreciation of the culture of one or two countries thanks to the time you will have spent living abroad as part of your degree course. A knowledge of a country's society, of cultural differences and of what sort of goods its inhabitants are likely to buy are important in marketing.

What skills are employers looking for?

Employers are looking for graduates with communication skills, initiative, numeracy, leadership, judgement, and a willingness to work as part of a team.

Sales personnel work at the sharp end. They travel to customers' or potential customers' premises to persuade them to buy a product. Export sales staff spend much of their time travelling. They need much the same skills as those required in marketing – except that they will not be working in a team. They will be on their own with the customer. Sales people need to be persevering, outgoing and good at mixing with all kinds of people.

Possible routes
* languages degree followed by postgraduate diploma course in marketing
* languages degree followed by a graduate traineeship with an employer
* degree or HND in business studies or marketing with languages.

☐ TOURISM

Tourism is now the UK's second largest industry and one which generates both jobs and revenue for Britain. Languages are an important asset here but, as in other jobs, they alone are not the key. The range of jobs is enormous: many demand the skills that would also be useful in marketing, advertising or public relations. The ones most likely to demand skill in languages are with the tour operators who take British holidaymakers abroad, with incoming tour operators and with the national and regional tourist boards which promote Britain overseas and encourage visitors to come here. Some people who are good at languages work as freelance guides showing people around Britain. All these jobs are described in *Working In Tourism* (see the book list in Chapter Sixteen).

☐ JOBS IN WHICH LANGUAGES CAN BE AN ASSET

Law

Many of the large law firms which practise in the City of London are part of international partnerships. Others have opened associate offices in key European cities. Several, for example, have decided to specialise in European Union law and have opened offices in Brussels. Solicitors who have a knowledge of languages have the opportunity to spend part of their career abroad or to travel frequently to continental Europe from their London base. Some law firms even let their trainees spend six months (of a two-year training period) in an overseas office. There are also jobs in the EU institutions.

The opportunities with law firms are for solicitors. But some barristers may work overseas also. Some are employed at the European Commission: others may travel occasionally to see clients on business.

Possible routes
• joint degree in law plus a language
• joint degree in law plus the law of another EU country plus a language
• law degree plus intensive language training.

Finance

Most banks have international divisions with branches in different countries. In general it is only managerial staff who get the opportunity to work overseas for a period since most staff are recruited locally. Accountants may work for firms which have associate offices in other countries. Many of the large firms are international companies which offer the opportunity to work in another country for a few years. Insurance companies have moved into other countries since the European single market was established in 1992. Brokers in particular may have the chance to travel since they may have to visit foreign clients. Obviously, the ability to conduct business in the client's language will be of benefit.

Librarianship

Librarians and information scientists are normally expected to have a knowledge of one or more foreign languages. This normally means a reading knowledge, however.

Journalism

Any journalist could be sent abroad at any time. There are also a few highly competitive vacancies for traineeships with the international news agency Reuters every year.

Plus
Transport (airlines, road and rail companies, shipping); freight forwarding; hotel management; the leisure industry; broadcasting

and the media; museum work; management consultancy; immigration officer work; customs and excise; market research. In all of these career areas the ability to communicate in a foreign language could prove useful. There are very few jobs nowadays in which languages are *not* an asset.

☐ LANGUAGES AS A GENERAL QUALIFICATION

It is important to know that not all language graduates enter employment directly related to their degree subject. Approximately 35 per cent of jobs notified to higher education institutions are suitable for students who have taken any subject. Language graduates enter these just as do students who have taken history, English, philosophy or any other humanities subject.

Latest figures available from higher education careers services (1993) show that of all the students who graduated in modern languages:

- 7.1% went on to further academic study
- 10.6% took teacher training courses
- 14.4% found employment abroad, usually teaching English.

Of those who found employment immediately in the UK:

- 20.6% entered sales, marketing and buying
- 18.8% went into administration and management
- 15.1% entered financial work
- 5.5% entered information, library and museum work
- 4.3% entered literary, creative and entertainment work
- 4.2% went into health and social welfare work.

The remainder went into a variety of jobs too small to categorise individually.

Some of the more unusual (as you might think for linguists) occupations included:

- accountancy
- advertising

- financial advice
- international banking
- management consultancy
- personnel work
- retail management.

(Source: *What do graduates do?*, Association of Graduate Careers Advisory Services.)

Chapter Two
WHICH LANGUAGE TO STUDY?

Which language or languages will you choose to study? The answer may seem obvious – those you are doing or have done for A-level. But you are not restricted to these. It is possible to start a new one in higher education. All you need is linguistic ability (proved by the fact that you know one or two languages already) plus, it must be said, a capacity for hard work! Beginners' courses are provided by many institutions. You would start off with an intensive introductory course. After a period spent abroad in a country where the language is spoken, you would find that you became fluent. It is easier to find beginners' courses in the less common languages, those not taught in many or any schools, but it is possible by judicious searching through higher education directories to find *some* in German and quite a number in Spanish. The one that is difficult to start from scratch is French. Because it is so widely taught in schools, most courses are set at post A-level standard, although there are a few courses possible for students who have a GCSE pass and just one or two for beginners.

At some universities and colleges which accept students from different language backgrounds, students are graded into three groups, post A-level, post GCSE and beginners – or *ab initio* to use the linguists' term. Teaching is done in these groups initially. Movement between them is allowed according to progress; sometimes the group structure is abandoned by the second year; and certainly by the final year when students have spent some time abroad, all initial differences have disappeared.

> *Remember, the more languages you study the easier it becomes to learn another.*

☐ HOW MANY LANGUAGES ARE TAUGHT IN UNIVERSITIES AND COLLEGES?

Far more than you would probably believe! Just take a look at this list.

Amharic, Arabic, Bengali, Bulgarian, Burmese, Cambodian, Catalan, Chinese, Croat, Czech, Danish, Dutch, Finnish, French, German, Gujarati, Greek, Hausa, Hebrew, Hindi, Indonesian, Italian, Japanese, Korean, Malay, Nepali, Norwegian, Occitan, Persian, Polish, Portuguese, Punjabi, Romanian, Russian, Serbian, Sinhalese, Slovak, Somali, Sotho, Spanish, Swahili, Swedish, Tamil, Thai, Tibetan, Turkish, Ukranian, Urdu, Vietnamese, Yoruba and IsiZulu.

Admittedly, many of these are probably of limited interest to most British students. However, should you feel like studying something really different, why not have a go? If you are interested in one of the more unusual languages you will find that it can be studied at only one or two places. The School of African and Oriental Studies and the School of Slavonic and East European Studies, both part of the University of London, are the only places where some are taught.

☐ WHICH LANGUAGES ARE MOST IN DEMAND?

French and German are still the leaders. 'Things have not changed much according to requests we get for information on language courses. People are studying French and German, with Spanish and Italian next,' says the Institute of Linguists. What people choose to study though could be entirely different from what is in demand! The Institute's findings are confirmed, however, by several London recruitment consultancies which specialise in placing secretary/administrators in commerce and industry. They find that employers ask for French first, followed by German. Spanish comes next, with Italian quite a long way behind in fourth place. They are noting however, increased demand for Russian, Japanese and Arabic.

The official languages of the UN are Arabic, Chinese, English, French, Russian and Spanish; those of the EU are Danish, Dutch,

English, Finnish, French, German, Greek, Italian, Portuguese, Spanish and Swedish.

☐ WHERE ARE THEY SPOKEN AND WHICH JOBS REQUIRE THEM?

French

France and her overseas territories, part of Belgium (Wallonia), parts of Switzerland, Canada, some African countries. More important than where it is spoken, however, is that it is widely used in business, is spoken in Brussels (together with Dutch), Luxembourg and Strasbourg where the EU institutions are located and is a second language for many people. French is an official UN language and is also the main language taught in British schools. Useful for industry/commerce/export, diplomatic work, teaching, general communication.

German

Germany, Austria, parts of Switzerland and widely understood as a second language in parts of Central and Eastern Europe. German is widely taught in British schools, sometimes as a second language after French, sometimes as the first foreign language. Many scientific texts are written in German.
Useful for industry/commerce/export, scientific translation work, teaching, general communication.

Spanish

Spain (which includes the Balearic and Canary Islands), Mexico, most South American countries. Spanish is an official UN language. Useful for industry/commerce/export, teaching, general communication. Particularly useful in tourism, given the numbers of British holidaymakers choosing Spain as a destination.

Italian

Italy and part of Switzerland.
Useful for industry/commerce/export, tourism. Less so for teaching since it is not widely taught in British schools.

Arabic

Most Middle Eastern countries and North African countries, including Egypt.
Arabic is becoming more useful in industry/commerce/export and is an official UN language. A knowledge could be helpful for TEFL teachers working in the Middle East.
NB The position of women in many Islamic countries means that job opportunities for women are restricted.

Japanese

Japan.
Becoming more useful in industry/commerce/export. A knowledge could be helpful for TEFL teachers since many Japanese people are keen to learn English.

Russian

Russia and the former countries of the USSR. A second language in many Eastern European countries and an official UN language.
Very important for industry/commerce/export. More British companies trade with Russia than ever before.

Chinese

China.
An official UN language. At the moment a knowledge of Chinese has rarity value. Trade with China is notoriously difficult. Only with time will it be possible to see whether trade will increase.

The question of which languages are the most useful is not easy to answer – in fact, you will notice if you have read this far that it has not been answered! The truth is that no one can predict with accuracy which languages will continue to be in demand or which ones might suddenly become so. The situation varies according to economic and political climates.

There is a case for equipping yourself with two major languages. The counter argument to that is that everyone else will do the same. There may seem little point in studying minority European languages such as Dutch, Greek or the Scandinavian languages since English is widely spoken in those countries, together with

French or German. However, remember the point made in Chapter One about speaking to customers in their own language. Also, Greek, like Italian, is useful in tourism.

If you study a language for its rarity value, you might find that there are few job opportunities in the year you qualify – and, as you will appreciate if you have read Chapter One, that any employer who wishes you to learn a particular language will normally pay for you to do so. The balancing argument to this is that the graduates who do study the unusual languages have little difficulty in finding alternative employment (see Chapter One) since many employers regard success in mastering a difficult language as an indication of general intellectual ability and determination.

Really, the answer is to study for interest. Choose a language you would like to learn and will enjoy. BUT bear the following in mind:

• If you are going to make a career as a serious linguist you will need more than one language.

• For general communication purposes, given that most people speak one of them as a second language, you should learn French, German or Spanish before opting for anything more exotic.

• If you discontinue the study of one of these after A-level in order to study another language, don't let it get rusty.

Chapter Three
DEGREE COURSES

Degree courses involving languages come in all shapes and sizes. You could choose to study one language alone, two, or even three. You could combine languages with the study of another subject. You could even do a course in engineering or computer science with a language. However, if one of these subjects is your major interest the language element will be more of an 'add-on'. You are more likely to want to read a book such as *Getting Into Engineering* or *Getting Into Computing*. This chapter will not cover courses in which language study is the minor element.

There are hundreds of courses. How are you going to make your choice? It is a question of priorities. What exactly are you hoping for from your course? If you have read Chapter One you will be aware that career opportunities to use languages alone are limited. If you choose a degree course which concentrates on languages without bringing in any other subjects or skills you will have to be prepared to:

- take a postgraduate course in, for example, business studies, tourism, hotel and hospitality management, translating
- look for a career as a graduate rather than as a languages graduate.

There is evidence that this message is getting across. Figures released by UCAS in relation to applications for entry in 1995 showed that there had been a decline in applications for pure languages degrees and an upsurge in applications for languages combined with business studies and other 'vocational' subjects.

However, the choice is yours. You must choose a course first and foremost that will interest you, but, if you do want to check out the career prospects, you could consult a careers adviser or simply find out what the graduates from a particular course are doing. Most prospectuses give some indication of jobs entered by their students.

☐ TYPES OF COURSE

It used to be relatively simple to define courses by the kind of institution that offered them. Older universities tended in the main to run what were regarded as 'traditional' courses, concentrating on the study of literature and the history and culture of the countries where the language was spoken. Many lectures were given in English and seminar and discussion classes also took place in English. Practical language skills might have been given as little as five hours per week. 'Applied' courses, offered by most of the former polytechnics and a handful of older universities, concentrated on language skills plus the life and institutions of the countries concerned. Literature was given a very small place and was sometimes omitted altogether.

This has changed. It would now be very unwise to attempt to classify courses in such a way. There has been a revolution in language teaching. Many of the older institutions have revised their syllabuses, conduct much of their teaching in the foreign language and offer optional courses in Business German, French for Journalism and so on. There is no short cut. You have to work your way through the prospectuses and decide for yourself which courses offer what *you* want.

Few people these days are willing to recommend certain places as offering the 'best' courses – because the questions are 'Best for what?' and 'Best for whom?' However, one professional organisation, the Institute of Translation and Interpreting, is prepared to suggest courses that will be 'of particular interest to would-be translators or interpreters'. These are at Bath, Bradford, Heriot-Watt, Kent, Kingston, UMIST, Salford, Surrey, Thames Valley and Westminster Universities.

☐ COMPARING COURSES

Which topics appear in language courses?

They all include four core skills:

- The written language, including grammar and vocabulary. Techniques used include essays, paraphrase and summary exercises. Translation, since it is a written exercise, may be included in this section. You would do *some* translation work on every course but at a few universities translation from English to a foreign language has been dropped.

- Speaking, listening comprehension and reading. Texts used for reading can include literature (poetry, plays, novels), periodicals, newspapers, political, social, economic and other contemporary documents. Language laboratories, satellite television and radio are used for improving aural skills and there are, of course, native speakers on the staff to help students to improve their oral work and to hold conversation classes.

The amount of time devoted to these language skills and the methods used to teach them vary from institution to institution.

In addition to the four core skills, you could find:

- in-depth study of literature, including analysis and textual criticism, with options offered to study writers from different periods, medieval to modern

- history and development of the language and linguistics - the study of the language itself and its structure

- translating and interpreting

- history of the country/ies where the language is spoken

- culture and thought of the countries

- economics of the country/ies

- politics and political institutions

- society – social structure, legal systems, religion, etc.

The above are the most usual topics. Within them you can often choose specialised options in cinema, theatre, gender studies, legal and other specialist language, art history and so on.

A very useful series of booklets which you could consult to compare and contrast syllabuses are the Degree Course Guides by CRAC.

They do much of the spade work for you by listing the specialisms of each degree course, the main topics studied and the number of hours devoted to each. They also tell you what proportion of lectures are given in the language you are studying.

If you look now at three very different French syllabuses, studied at different universities, you will appreciate how important it is to do this research very carefully, rather than assuming that all degree courses are the same!

University A

Compulsory Units
> French Language
> Advanced French Usage
> French Society 1914- present
> Introduction to French Literature
> The Arts in Contemporary France
> The French Language in the Modern World
> One unit taken from another subject (wide choice).

Optional Units
> French Society 1789-1914
> French Novel
> French Literature of Ideas
> French Poetry
> French Drama
> French Society under the *Ancien Régime*
> History of the French Language
> Modern Critical Theory
> French Renaissance Literature
> Old French Literature
> Renaissance Literature
> Comic Drama 1550-1789
> The Romantic Era
> The Second Empire
> Realist Fiction
> Avant-Garde and Modernism
> Recent Currents in French Thought
> Politics into Literature
> Romance Linguistics
> Love Poetry from Renaissance to Romanticism
> Racine and 17th-century Tragedy

Drama and Performance in 17th-century France
The 17th-century French Novel
18th-century French Political Thought
19th-century French Theatre
The Romantic Personal Narrative
Balzac and his Contemporaries
The Symbolists
Literary Reflections of the Dreyfus Affair
Surrealism
Literature and Political Activism
Sartre
20th-century French Theatre
French Cinema
Chanson Francaise
Modern Developments in French and German Fiction
The Francophone Literature of Black Africa and the West
Indies
The Novel in Action
Developments in Present-day French.

University B

NB This particular university does not offer French as a single
subject. It must be combined with another – not necessarily a
language. The courses listed therefore represent only 50 per cent
of a student's workload.

Compulsory Units
French Language
Introduction to Contemporary France.

Optional Units
The Business Environment in France
Education and Society in France
Women in French Society
Mass Media and the State in France
World War Two: The French Experience
The Right in France
The Trade Union Movement and the Left in France
Politics and Society in France since 1945
Economic Policy in Contemporary France
Rural France
Independent Study
Dissertation.

University C

This degree is in Modern Languages (two of French, German, Russian, Spanish).

Compulsory Units
Structure of Language
Society and Culture of Two Countries
Translation
Interpreting
Written Expression.

Optional Units
Third Language (Dutch, Italian, Portuguese)
TEFL
Economics/Politics/Literature (of one or more countries)
Catalan
Franco-German Relations
International Politics
Romance Linguistics
Translation Theory
Women in Russia.

☐ COURSES IN MORE THAN ONE LANGUAGE

On **dual language** courses the language elements of the syllabus are usually the same for each language. There is obviously a smaller amount of time for additional topics. You would choose some from each subject and would tailor them to your own interests. Timetable clashes might mean that not all your chosen options could be taken but there is normally a sufficiently wide choice to cater for most people's interests.

Depending on the structure of the course, you might choose an equal number of optional units from both subjects or give a slight emphasis to one, choosing for instance, more units from topics in German literature, society and culture than from French.

On courses involving **three** languages (popular with students who wish to continue with two A-level languages and begin another) it is usual to 'major' in two and study the third to a less advanced level.

☐ COMBINED COURSES

You could study a modern foreign language in combination with any of the following on a degree course:

Accountancy
African Studies
American Studies
Banking
Business Studies
Cartography
Catering Management
Classical Studies
Communication Studies
Computing
Dance
Drama
Ecology
Economics
Fine Art
Food Science
Geography
Geology
History
History of Art
Housing
Human Resources Management
Law
Librarianship and Information Studies
Marketing
Mathematics
Media studies
Music
Philosophy
Planning
Politics
Psychology
Sociology
Sports Studies
Theology
Tourism
Victorian Studies
War Studies
Women's Studies.

(There are also courses in biology, chemistry, physics, paper science and engineering combined with a language.)

The content of any of the above courses must be checked very carefully. When elements of two courses are put together something has to go. As you would be doing 50 per cent of each syllabus you would need to read the prospectuses and course leaflets in detail to establish whether the optional units available in a single-subject course that interest you are also available on a two subject course. At one place they might not; at another they might be. Much depends on the timetable.

Some combined/joint courses are literally that – two parts of two syllabuses slotted together to cater for students who want to study both subjects. Others are planned as a whole. These tend to be the courses with a proportion of professional training in them. Notable examples are law and business studies in combination with languages.

☐ LAW WITH LANGUAGES

These courses are very popular but you do need to know what you are applying for. Some are courses in English/Scots law with the additional study of a language. Others are joint degrees covering the legal systems of two countries and involving study in each.

If you chose Law with German, you could give yourself a thorough grounding in English/Scots law, take some options in German and/or EU law and spend part of your course in Germany, perfecting your German. If you chose Law with German *Law* you would study the law of both countries. Students on such courses spend half of the course at a university in each country and gain a qualification in both legal systems. (NB A law degree, however, must always be followed by further training before you can practise law.)

☐ BUSINESS AND MANAGEMENT STUDIES

The emphasis can also vary on these courses. There are different courses for those who want to make languages the main or equal (even minor) part of the degree. On all of them you would study the basic business subjects: accountancy, law, economics. All courses contain options – the ones combined with languages tend to emphasise those like marketing, European business, international finance etc.

You could study one language or two, sometimes three – and all your language work would be done in a business context. Most courses give you one year in another country, in a business placement, at a higher education institution or in a combination of the two. On a smaller number you would spend two years in the UK and two years in another country. The most popular of these are the ones which send their students abroad twice, once as a student at a partner university; once to work in commerce or industry. Once again, prospectuses and course leaflets must be read carefully in order to compare what is on offer.

If you have got to the end of this chapter you cannot have avoided picking up the fact that courses vary and that you do have to research them with care!

To summarise the various sources of help available:

Use
• Degree Course Guides
• *Degree Course Offers*
• *University and College Entrance*
• University and college prospectuses
• Departmental course and subject leaflets.

Consult
• Language teachers
• Careers advisers.

Everyone talks about degree courses, right? Did you know that there is an alternative course in higher education – one that (most important) also attracts a mandatory grant? Higher National Diploma (HND) courses exist in a range of subjects, some of which are of particular relevance to people wanting to incorporate some language study in their course.

HND courses are widely recognised by employers. Some courses, depending on the area of study, give their holders - known as *diplomates* – exemption from certain professional examinations.

It is very difficult to equate HNDs directly with degree courses and often misleading to try to do so. However, you'll want to know what such a qualification is worth. Some employers regard the diplomas as the equivalent of a pass degree, others slightly lower; while some do not worry about equivalents. They regard it as a qualification in its own right and look at the course content when considering applicants for jobs. It is only fair to point out, though, that there are employers who recruit graduates only.

☐ WHAT IS AN HND?

- A qualification validated by either BTEC (Business and Technology Education Council) in England and Wales or SCOTVEC (Scottish Vocational Education Council) in Scotland. BTEC and SCOTVEC *validate* courses, rather than set the syllabus. An institution wishing to offer a HND programme must submit its syllabus to one of them for approval.

- A vocational course. The HND course is always linked to the world of work. It contains work experience and practical assignments. Before courses are validated, BTEC and SCOTVEC make sure that the vocational content of the course is suitable, that lecturers have appropriate qualifications and experience, that the institution has the resources to run the course and that employers have been consulted in drawing up the programme.

• It is designed to prepare students for supervisory or managerial level employment.

• It gives a practical qualification which means that its holders should be able to contribute as soon as they enter employment.

It's important to know however, before you read on, that you won't find HNDs in French or in languages. They are always *applied* courses. You *will* find courses with titles like European Business Studies, European Marketing and Business Studies.

☐ DIFFERENCES BETWEEN HND AND DEGREE COURSES

1. HNDs take a year less to complete than a degree in a similiar subject. They last two years on a full-time basis or three if a sandwich year is included.

2. They are offered in:

• the newest universities (the former polytechnics) but not in traditional ones
• some colleges and institutes of higher education
• some colleges of further education.

3. The entry requirements are lower. Technically, you need one of the following:

• one A-level pass
• two AS-levels
• two Highers
• pass level in a national diploma or GNVQ advanced diploma.

In practice, however, higher grades are normally demanded – just as the minimum entry requirements to a degree course are two A-level grade Es but very few people are accepted with these grades.

To be quite honest, the reason why some students choose HND courses is that the entry grades are lower! It is not a good idea to do so though, unless you have checked the course content and know what is involved. If your heart is set on a literary-based degree in French and Spanish, you may not be happy on a HND course in European Marketing which has these two languages as minor subjects.

Just as when choosing a degree course, it is important to look at syllabuses and ask questions.

HND courses which may be of interest to language students

Business and Finance
Business and Finance (Export Management)
Business Studies
European Business Studies
European Studies
Hotel and Catering (Hospitality) Management*
International Marketing
European Business Administration.
Travel and Tourism.

* Languages will form a very minor part of this course.

☐ TYPICAL COURSE CONTENTS

HND Business and Finance

Year 1

Compulsory Units
Business environment
Business functions
Accounting
The individual and the organisation
Quantitative information systems.

Optional Units
Marketing
Manpower
International business
Languages

Self employment
Office administration.

Year 2

Compulsory Units
Financial management
Management information systems
Languages
Operations management
Finance
Business policy.

HND Business Studies with Tourism

Year 1

Information processing
Organisation behaviour
(40% of time)

Travel and tourism
Travel and tourism geography
Spanish or French

Year 2

Management information
People and organisations
(50%)

Travel and tourism
Marketing
French or Spanish.

Year 3

Strategic analysis
Human resource management
Quality management
(60%)

Tourism and transport
Either French, Spanish or economics.

Plus 20 weeks' work experience which may be spent abroad.

HND European Business Studies

Years 1 and 3

Business environment
Organisation studies
Information analysis
European business environment
Marketing
Two of French, German, Spanish
Business resources
Corporate policy.

This is a three-year course, with the second year spent studying business studies or international trade at a business school in France, Germany or Spain.

HND Hotel, Catering and Institutional Management

Year 1

Compulsory Units

Provision of food and drink
Marketing
Hotel and catering environment
Rooms division operations
Behaviour in organisations
Human behaviour
Management accounting
Management of IT
European language.

Optional Units

Nutrition and microbiology
Food technology
The food chain
Tourism and leisure
Information systems.

Year 2

Supervised work experience.

Year 3

Compulsory Units

Food and beverage management

Management accounting
Human resources management
Project
Management practices
Second European language.

Optional Units
Catering systems
Advanced food hygiene
Food processing
Management strategy
Financial management
Consumer behaviour
Market research
Tourism and leisure
Licensed house management
Contract catering
Small business management
Gastronomy.

Plus a one-week field course in continental Europe.

☐ WHAT DO PEOPLE DO AT THE END OF A HND COURSE?

• Start work

• Transfer to the final year of a degree course in a related field

• Take a postgraduate course.

Chapter Five
SECRETARIAL COURSES

Choosing a bi-lingual secretarial course must be done with care. Some are little more than secretarial courses with a few hours of weekly language tuition tacked on. Some offer you the opportunity to gain a basic or working knowledge of two, even three languages; others concentrate on one. Some include shorthand in a foreign language; others in English only.

Whichever you choose, it is important to realise that you are training to work as a *secretary/administrator* – not as a translator or a public relations executive or an export manager. Yes, these careers may develop later. Yes, some people use a secretarial course to gain experience in a chosen field, then make the cross-over to a different level of work – later. But initially, there is no getting away from the fact that the course is going to contain the basic skills of secretarial work: typing/word processing, shorthand and office procedures.

Even if your thinking is to take a secretarial course as a stepping stone, do be prepared to express some interest in these subjects at a college interview – and don't be surprised if you get a slightly frosty reception if you don't! Do remember too, that the job of a bi-lingual secretary is, for many people, interesting in itself and that the work often involves a good deal of correspondence translation, telephone work and meeting and looking after foreign visitors.

☐ DIFFERENT COURSES

Secretarial course with language option

This is a fairly representative syllabus of courses held in many state colleges of further education. Everyone studies:

- typing
- audio-typing   } beginners, intermediate, advanced
- word processing
- shorthand or CLAIT (computer literacy and information

technology – spreadsheets, databases)
* business administration.

Students then choose either a medical secretarial, legal secretarial, book-keeping or languages option. Languages students study either French, German or Spanish and take language examinations for London Chamber of Commerce and Industry (LCCI) or Royal Society of Arts (RSA) certificates.

The course lasts one or two years depending on students' entry qualifications and prior knowledge.

You may or may not be required to speak in your foreign language or even be interviewed at all for such courses. Some admissions tutors are happy to rely on school reports and pay particular attention to language teachers' assessments of ability.

Similar courses exist in private colleges. They are usually shorter (one year). Again, the amount of time devoted to language study varies. Some offer additional classes at extra cost for students who wish to specialise further in languages.

RSA Higher Diploma in Administrative and Secretarial Procedures

This course is an intensive preparation for students who want to become PAs or senior secretaries. The syllabus covers:

* typing
* audio-typing
* word processing
* shorthand
* information processing
* business administration.

Students learn to organise and administer meetings, arrange business travel, analyse financial information, plan and set up conferences – either in real situations or as simulations. Students may take a language option. In this case many of the practical tasks are carried out in a foreign language. They may also take LCCI Euroqualifications.

However, the actual language input is not very high. Students are almost always required to have a very good knowledge before commencing the course. Many are graduates or have equivalent level qualifications.

Courses which carry out some of their teaching in a foreign language

These are held in some state colleges, in some independent or private ones and in a number of the newer universities (former polytechnics). Some universities now run HND courses in secretarial procedures with languages. It's worth checking these out because HND courses qualify for mandatory grants. (See Chapter Fifteen).

Many courses last for one year only and presuppose a very high standard of linguistic fluency. Like the RSA Higher Diploma course, they are often more suitable for graduates or people who have lived and worked abroad.

A truly bi-lingual course is offered by the French Institute, or College de Secrétariat Bilingue de l'Institut Français du Royaume-Uni, the official French Government Centre of language and culture in London. Students with degree level or equivalent French may take a one year course. There is however, a second course for students with A-level or equivalent knowledge. If you took the two-year course your weekly timetable would consist of 28 hours, broken down like this:

English shorthand, typing, word processing and secretarial procedures	10 hours
French shorthand and typing	5 hours
Written and spoken French	5 hours
French and English business correspondence and commercial translation	3 hours
Contemporary France and Europe	2 hours
English and French business studies	3 hours.

In the second year there are three hours of commercial French and one of commercial English and two of business studies in French.

You would also do a four week work experience placement with a firm in the UK or abroad.

Successful completion of the course leads to the award of a diploma from the University of Lille.

The one-year course is more intensive – 33 hours per week, with the additional five hours being spent on basic secretarial skills (typing, shorthand, etc).

Students are always interviewed for places on these courses. If you applied for the two-year course your language skills would also be tested through two-way translation and exercises in written French.

Although the Institute is a private establishment, due to the level and content of the course, *some* local education authorities do give students discretionary grants to attend it. More, however, pay their own fees but are able to claim 25 per cent tax relief for vocational training.

There is now one degree course in secretarial studies – at Northumbria University, Newcastle. Foreign languages and work experience abroad are offered as an option on this syllabus.

A useful book, *The Guide to Training in Secretarial and Office Skills*, by Angela Mortimer plc in conjunction with Hobsons Publishing plc was written in Spring 1995. A free copy was sent to every secondary school. If you are still at school, you should be able to find it in your careers library.

Chapter Six
SHORT COURSES

Short courses do not train professional linguists and should not be seen as a short cut by people hoping to make major use of languages in a career – that is, as teachers, translators or interpreters.

They are extremely useful when used for the right purposes however. They can:

* serve as an introduction to a language

* be tailored to fulfil a particular need.

Into the first group come courses geared to beginners who want to learn a language for leisure purposes or as a taster to see whether or not they enjoy it. If so, they might decide to continue with more in-depth study. Into the second come the intensive and total immersion courses aimed at people who will be going abroad to live or who will be travelling frequently to other countries. The courses do work – because the students are going to put the languages into practice at once and to continue learning in an active environment. It is generally accepted that if you take a concentrated course you must put the language into practice immediately. Otherwise you soon begin to forget what you have learned. The more quickly you learn a language, the faster you lose it.

Short courses can also benefit people who want a working knowledge of a language for use in their jobs in this country – if they are required to use the language frequently. They too can continue to learn and practise.

Intensive language courses are for people in a hurry. They are usually taken by business executives needing to acquire competence in a language quickly before beginning to make business trips to a new country. They may be taken by executives who are going to be posted abroad, where they will be in charge of an organisation and will need sufficient language knowledge to work and survive there 24 hours a day. Government departments like the Foreign and

Commonwealth Office also teach their staff by means of intensive tuition.

Where you study will depend on your requirements, on the amount of time you have and on the price you can afford. Courses are not cheap. At one end of the scale are the total immersion courses aimed at the person needing to learn a language in as little as one month. (All teaching is conducted in the language being studied, from lesson one; students may have as many as seven hours' daily tuition, spend lunchtime with a tutor and be given homework.) Such courses are available at around £1200-£1500 per week plus VAT. At the other end are the evening or lunchtime classes held in small groups, costing on average £4 – £6 per hour.

Before enrolling any student, a school will conduct a short test. You would be asked questions in the language itself if you were not a beginner, or in any other language you knew, so that the tutor could assess your present level and your ability to respond to changes in tense and mood. They would ask how many languages you knew already and at what level, in order to estimate how long it would take you to learn the one you wish to study. For example, if you had already done some Russian or another less common language they would, like the university admissions tutors mentioned in Chapter Nine, take this as an indication that you might need fewer than the average number of hours to master another difficult language. They would also establish your exact requirements. Do you for instance, want to be able to communicate? To speak fluently? To write ? and so on.

☐ HOW DO YOU FIND A SCHOOL?

There is no nationally compiled list. Most schools advertise locally in their *Yellow Pages* or you may hear of one through recommendation. One guarantee of standards is to choose one which is a member of ALEX, the Association of Language Excellence Centres (this does not imply that non-ALEX members do not offer quality teaching). You can also obtain recommendations from the Information or Cultural Sections of most embassies and consulates. They will either assist or refer you to another source. Where German is concerned, you would find the Goethe Institut helpful. They publish details of language courses run by the Institute in England and in Germany. Similarly

for French courses, you could contact the Alliance Française, for
Spanish, the Instituto Cervantes, and for Italian the Italian
Institute. All addresses can be found in Chapter Sixteen.

☐ STUDY COURSES ABROAD

There are some excellent courses held in most countries. These give
you the opportunity to absorb some of the life and culture of the
country while you are learning. All lengths of course are available
from one week upwards, with social, cultural and sporting activities
often included. Many courses are run during school and college
holidays so that students of any age can benefit.

The usual pattern is to choose a package of 15, 20 or more hours
of tuition with social activities on top and to choose whether to be
accommodated in hotels, apartments or with families. The most
successful method is to opt for half- or full-board with a family.
There are even some courses held in the teacher's home. Under
this method students speak the language at all times.

Examples

• 10–40 hours of Spanish tuition per week. Optional homework. Use
  of video, computer and language laboratories. Courses in history
  and culture available. Plus a creative workshop for would-be
  authors to write in Spanish. One-day and half-day excursions
  each week to historic sites. Access to sports facilities such as
  swimming and tennis arranged. Bed and breakfast or full-board
  accommodation available with Spanish families. Courses held all
  year round.

• Three hours of instruction in French each day plus additional
  lessons in vocabulary, grammar, phonetics and history and
  culture. Students may live in the school's premises, with families
  or in private lodgings. Programmes last from one to ten weeks.

• 20 hours each week of tuition in Italian plus optional twice weekly
  afternooon courses in history of art, current affairs, Italian wines,
  etc. Excursions to museums, galleries and towns in the region.
  Sporting activities arranged on request. Full board with local
  families.

There are many, many variations on the above themes and something somewhere to suit everyone. Prices are impossible to quote since they depend on the exact package taken.

☐ HOW DO YOU FIND A LANGUAGE SCHOOL ABROAD?

They often advertise in British newspapers - or use agents who place the advertisements and help to find students for them. You can also find information on some schools in:

Teenager's Vacation Guide to Work, Study and Adventure, published by Vacation Work.

Study Holidays, Central Bureau for Educational Visits and Exchanges.

Chapter Seven
POSTGRADUATE COURSES

If your languages course does not include translating and interpreting techniques, and you are hoping to work as an interpreter and/or translator, you would be well advised to consider taking a course of professional training. You will also need to look carefully at the course content. Interpreting and translating are very different skills. Although a number of interpreters can also translate, says the Institute of Linguists, few, if any, translators by training can act as interpreters.Which do you want to specialise in?

☐ COURSES AVAILABLE

There are several of these courses; some held in other countries. You can obtain their addresses from the Institute of Translation and Interpreting.

As far as courses in this country are concerned the Institute lists the following:

Translation studies

> University of Bath
> University of Bradford
> Heriot-Watt University, Edinburgh
> University of Kent
> University of Salford
> University of Surrey
> UMIST (University of Manchester Institute of Science and
> Technology)
> University of Westminster.

These universities also offer courses in Conference interpreting/ technical translation. UMIST offers a course in machine translating and Westminster has separate courses for translation and interpreting.

Literary translation

University of Essex.

☐ COURSE CONTENT

What would you study? What do you need to study in addition to language itself?

The answer to the second question is that you need training in the skills of both professions, in technical vocabulary and lots of practice under simulated conditions. Even naturally bi-lingual students say they have benefited from practising, for example, conference interpreting, in the conditions they would find in an interpreter's booth.

A translation syllabus

(This is taken from one of the above courses.)

One year course: two languages

Translation Practice: economics, politics, law, technology
Aspects of Law
Principles of Economics
Electro-mechanical Technology
Translation Theory and Methods
Stylistics
Word Processing
Computerised Aids to Translation.

Students are assessed on coursework, on an extended translation and by examination.

Interpreting

Interpreting syllabuses cover similar ground but with very different emphasis.

They stress the spoken word and the techniques of simultaneous and consecutive interpreting. Courses are very hard work. Students comment on the fact that they have 25 hours of classes each week and are expected to do additional work in their 'free' time.

☐ INSTITUTE OF LINGUISTS DIPLOMA IN TRANSLATION

Examinations for the Institute's Diploma in Translation, which is at postgraduate level, are held in November each year. Three written papers are taken in general translation; one of technology, business or literature; and one of science or humanities. All three papers must be passed in order for the diploma to be awarded. Forty different language combinations are available. Courses leading to the diploma are available at several universities and colleges. It is also possible to study through distance learning via the National Extension College. Further details from the Institute.

Chapter Eight
THE YEAR ABROAD

On practically all languages degree courses students are expected to spend one academic year abroad – normally the third – in a country where their language/s of study are spoken. Even in the small number of universities and colleges where this is not an integral part of the course, it is usually highly recommended that students should do so.

☐ THE CHOICES AVAILABLE

There are three basic patterns. Each has its advantages and disadvantages.

1. To go abroad as a student. If you took this option, you would be enrolled as a student at a university or similar establishment that has links with your own. You would attend lecture courses suggested by your home institution and may be assigned to a member of academic staff who will keep an eye on you. Arrangements are often made under the EU ERASMUS programme (see Chapter Fourteen).

Advantages:

• You know where you are going.

• Some arrangements are made on your behalf (although this can be as little as the issue of addresses, names and directions).

• You may be able to live in student accommodation – but this is not as plentiful as it is in the UK.

• You are going to a familiar environment.

• You should be able to make friends with local students and other native speakers.

• You will have a lot of free time.

46

Disadvantages

Poverty! You may receive an addition to your grant during the time spent abroad, but it rarely covers everything.

2. To work as an foreign language assistant in a school.

Advantages

- You will be paid a salary, admittedly not magnificent, but it will be more to live on than a grant.

- Accommodation will probably be found for you.

- The English teacher/s will take an interest in you. They may meet you on arrival, introduce you to friends, look after you until you find your feet.

Disadvantages

- You will follow a planned weekly timetable with no days off. You will have the holidays though for independent travel.

- You will have to put some effort into making friends of your own age.

- You will be expected to speak English for a number of hours each week.

- You may dislike teenagers/teaching.

3. To go on a work placement in industry or commerce.

Advantages

- Money.

- Real work experience.

- Maturity. You will learn to stand on your own feet.

Disadvantages

- You will be much more on your own and be responsible for establishing a social life.

Students taking applied language courses or ones which combine languages with business studies usually spend a period abroad in a work placement. Sometimes they spend two six month periods abroad, one as a student and one at work.

You may have the option of doing any of the above since some British institutions are flexible and allow students to choose which kind of year abroad they wish to do. Others do not. Or they may not have enough links to be able to give everyone their preference. It is something worth considering when you start to read prospectuses – and you could ask what the arrangements are if you are invited to an interview.

- What is the approved arrangement?

- Who makes the arrangements, you or staff?

- Which countries and which regions could you choose from?

- How is the year financed?

- How have previous students found the experience? (Not all students enjoy it, unfortunately. But for every one who comes back complaining of a boring placement or an unfriendly school there are many more who have a marvellous time and count the year abroad as one of the best parts of their course.)

You may have no preference at the moment as to how you spend a period abroad, but if you do, be sure that you know how the system works at the universities/colleges you are going to apply to.

Chapter Nine
BEGINNING A NEW LANGUAGE

So you are going to learn a new language. How difficult will that be
– given that you will be expected to reach degree level in four years
as though you had taken A-level? How gifted do you need to be? Can
you assess your aptitude in advance? Would it be wiser to stick to
French?

☐ DIFFICULTY?

There is no denying that some languages are easier than others –
depending on your previous language base. The group which
developed from Latin, for instance, have much in common. If you
speak French, Spanish and Italian should come pretty easily and
once you have done either Italian or Spanish the other should
present no difficulty. Romanian belongs to the same family. Dutch
is not difficult for speakers of English and German.

☐ A LESS COMMON LANGUAGE

Dr Nigel Phillips teaches Indonesian at London University's School
of Oriental and African Studies. He says, 'It is bound to be harder
initially than learning some new languages because there is no
common stock of vocabulary – no easily recognisable words other
than loan words such as "taxi" or "telephone". Happily, it is
nowadays written in Roman script and it does not contain any
sounds that the average British tongue finds impossible to
pronounce. The grammar is relatively simple; tenses are easy and
there are no genders or cases such as you get in German to worry
about. Nor does it have tones like some oriental languages.'

☐ DIFFERENT ALPHABETS

These are not as problematical as they look. If you are going to try Russian or Greek, yes, you have to learn a new alphabet, but that doesn't take very long and once you have mastered it, it is no harder to learn the grammar and constructions involved than in some languages which use the same characters as English.

At universities where beginners may take Russian, they look for ability in any foreign language as a guide to aptitude. A good predicted grade in any language is the key – plus enthusiasm. *One* modern foreign language at A-level is the usual minimum, but most admissions tutors would be happier to see two – at GCSE if not at A-level. Passes in Latin and Greek are also seen as helpful, so if your school still teaches classical languages and you have chosen to take them, don't see this as a wasted step. They are widely regarded as more difficult languages and furthermore, give a good base in grammar and complex constructions.

☐ DIFFERENT SCRIPTS

These do look difficult! But again, say people who teach them, they are not as difficult as you might think. The first few weeks are the hardest until the script has been learned. Dr Nigel Phillips again, this time on Malay. 'Malay has been described as "bafflingly easy". This means that although the language seems simple at an early stage, complications – mainly in the form of prefixes and suffixes – do arise after a while and may take a little time to master.'

Dr Phillips' department does not set aptitude tests of any kind but does look for genuine enthusiasm for Asian languages. On the whole, they are happier to accept students who have done *some* language learning previously – at GCSE or A-level.

Rupert Snell teaches Hindi. He says, 'The script is phonetically organised and surprisingly straightforward to learn. The process is not unlike learning shorthand. The grammar is no more complicated than that of European languages. Anyone who has successfully learned a language such as French or German should have no great difficulty.'

Chapter Ten
CHOOSING WHERE TO APPLY

You will have already seen in Chapters Three to Five that one of the most important things to do when choosing any course involving languages is to check its content very carefully.

You won't be happy if you end up on the wrong course. It *is* possible to change, but you may lose a year and have to wait for the next applications cycle if you leave it too late. You could also have grant problems if you spent more than 20 weeks on a course before deciding that you had made a mistake. So it pays to get it right.

Academic matters are not the only consideration however. What else should you think about ?

Well, you are going to be spending several years at the institution you finally choose, so it is important that you are happy there. This means looking at several factors.

☐ THE ENVIRONMENT, THE SURROUNDINGS AND THE ATMOSPHERE

1. Are you a town mouse or a country mouse? Do you love big cities or prefer the countryside?

2. Do you want a campus university/college?

3. Do you mind if the institution is on more than one site?

4. Should it be large or small?

5. What kind of accommodation would you prefer?

The usual alternatives are:

- halls of residence providing some meals
- self-catering hall
- bed and breakfast or half-board accommodation locally
- renting private accommodation.

6. What kind of social and sporting facilities are there?

7. How far from home are you prepared to go?

How to find out

Consult:
- Prospectus
- Departmental or subject handbook
- Video – if available
- ECCTIS.

Ask for a copy of the accommodation handbook.
Go to Open Days if possible.

☐ WHAT ABOUT TEACHING AND ASSESSMENT METHODS?

1. Are there many lectures?

2. What is the average seminar group size?

3. How many of the staff are native speakers ?

4. Does the department use continuous assessment and/or examinations?

5. Do you spend a period abroad?

How to find out

Consult:
- Degree Course Guides
- Prospectus
- Departmental or subject handbook.

☐ CAN YOU GET IN?

1. What entry grades would you need?

How to find out

Consult:
- *University and College Entrance*
- Prospectus.

☐ THE COST

1. How much will it cost to get there each term (or semester)?

2. What is the cost of accommodation?

The cost of accomodation can vary considerably. The National Union of Students carried out a comprehensive survey of accommodation costs last year. There was £39 *per week* difference in rents charged by the most expensive and cheapest institutions for a single room in self-catering accommodation. In general, costs are higher in London and the South-east.

How to find out

Consult:
- British Rail, coach company or parents (!) Could they take you by car?
- Ask for a copy of the accommodation handbook.

The number of applications you may make for courses in any one year is limited. You may make only six UCAS applications. (This covers most degree and HND courses.) You may however, apply to as many courses that do not recruit through UCAS (eg private colleges, secretarial courses) as you wish.

Given the small permitted number of UCAS courses, you can't afford to waste an application. Therefore, before you start to fill in any application forms, you need to know as much as possible about the universities, colleges and courses you are considering. You will be using various criteria to make your selection, hopefully including some of those outlined in Chapter Ten. Fortunately, there are several different ways of getting the necessary information.

☐ PROSPECTUSES

These are the glossy booklets produced by universities and colleges. They are essentially public relations as well as information exercises – they are out to attract you to come, so they are not going to mention their bad points! Much time and effort goes into producing them and they are quite expensive. One university admissions officer estimates £3.00 per copy. To you they are free.

A prospectus should contain a description of each course, saying how it is organised, how students' work is assessed and what the entry requirements are. (Sometimes these entries are briefer but you are invited to send for a specific course leaflet.) It also describes social, sporting and welfare facilities and accommodation. Throughout are photographs to help you decide whether you might like the place.

You should acquire lots of these. You can do so either by phoning, sending a postcard (addresses and phone numbers are in the UCAS handbook) or pick some up at a higher education fair. More on these below.

☐ ALTERNATIVE PROSPECTUSES

These are produced by student unions in many universities and colleges and can be obtained from them on request. They are meant to give the students' views, are often interesting to say the least, and make quite good reading. They can be less comprehensive and give only the viewpoint of the student author so they are best read in conjunction with the official prospectus.

☐ VIDEOS OR VIDEO PROSPECTUSES

These are as glossy as the prospectuses and always present a very positive image. Nevertheless, they can be useful in giving you some feel for the place. Your school or college may have reference copies – or you can sometimes borrow them yourself from the institutions.

☐ HIGHER EDUCATION FAIRS

These are held in many parts of the country, usually in the late spring or the summer term because they are designed for Year 12 pupils who have already been given some basic information on higher education by their school staff. They are like big trade fairs or the careers conventions you may be used to, with representatives from most higher education institutions taking a stand. They are an opportunity to collect prospectuses and leaflets, but more than that. You should also be able to ask any questions you have and to get advice. (It's worth making out a list of questions before you go.) UCAS and private secretarial colleges usually have stands too.

Most schools and colleges take parties of pupils to them, but if nothing is being organised for you, you can always go independently. Most fairs run over into the weekend and they are advertised in the national newspapers.

☐ OPEN DAYS

These offer a real opportunity to get a proper look at the place where you might be going to spend the next few years. Do try and get to them. Yes, it's expensive but would you buy a car because of its brochure description without test driving it or an outfit without trying it on?

So much for the non-academic side of things.

To help you narrow down your choice of course and make a reasonable shortlist without having to wade through dozens of prospectuses, you could use the CRAC Degree Course Guides. These compare the syllabuses at all the different higher education institutions and tell you what proportion of time is spent on the different topics and if certain topics are even included at all. With a subject like modern languages, where the approach at different institutions does vary so much, the guides can be invaluable. Armed with a pen, paper and a list of your priorities you can look for the courses with, say, the smallest amount of linguistics, the greatest amount of time devoted to translation, the opportunity to study the contemporary cinema in the country where the language is spoken, to study one author in depth and so on. The guides also cover assessment methods.

For entry requirements you really need *University and College Entrance,* or *Degree Course Offers* (available from Trotman & Co Ltd).

☐ PEOPLE

One of the most important sources of information is other people. Lots of them are able to give advice.

- Your subject teacher who knows your strengths and weaknesses.

- Your head of sixth form, careers adviser, head of upper school – whoever organises higher education applications. They attend conferences and open days and are bound to have visited many colleges and universities.

- Staff from higher education institutions who may come in to give information talks.

- Students from your school/college who have gone before you.

- Friends, relatives, anyone who has studied at any place you might be interested in. (Be sure their information is up to date!)

Badger any and all of these for information.

There is a full list of reference books in Chapter Sixteen.

☐ UCAS

UCAS, the Universities and Colleges Admissions Service, which is
based in Cheltenham, handles admissions for degree, Dip HE and
higher national diploma courses. It charges you a fee (currently
£12.00 or £4.00 should you apply to only one course) for processing
the applications and passes on decisions from universities and
colleges to you, but its staff make no decisions themselves. That is
up to individual admissions tutors. UCAS in effect acts as a mailbox.

How UCAS works

You obtain a form from your school or college or, if you have left, by
writing to UCAS in the autumn term, a year ahead of entry. You
may apply from 1 September and the closing date for receipt of
applications is 15 December, unless you are applying to Oxford or
Cambridge, in which case the closing date is 15 October. (If you
apply later, UCAS will still process your application but universities
and colleges are not obliged to consider it if they have already
received a large number of applications.) You may choose a
maximum of six courses, which may be a combination of degree and
HND courses.

For full details of how the system is organised and advice on
completing the form, you should consult another book in this
series, *How to Complete Your UCAS Form*. What follows is a brief
summary.

Timetable

You fill in the form and hand it with your cheque or postal order to
cover the applicant's fee to the person who writes the references in
your school or college. (Mature applicants are asked to provide a
reference from someone able to write about their academic ability.)
You do not see the form again since the reference is supposed to be
confidential!

Your referee posts the form and within a few weeks you should get an acknowledgement from UCAS and your personal application number. If you don't hear within two or three weeks you should check that the form has arrived in Cheltenham. You may do this yourself by phoning or ask your referee to do so. UCAS stresses, however, that you need to know when the form was *posted* before you start to worry. Some schools may take several weeks to process the forms if they are writing large numbers of references.

UCAS sends reduced size copies of your form to all your chosen institutions. Each considers you and tells UCAS whether they are offering you a place and what the conditions are. (That you get certain grades in the forthcoming examinations are the usual ones but occasionally they might ask you to get an additional GCSE pass if you are retaking a subject to make up your passes to the minimum number.) This is known as a *conditional offer*. If you have already taken A-levels or equivalent exams you can be made an unconditional offer
(that is, offered a firm place) because your results are known.

Interviews are not given as frequently as they used to be, partly because of the cost to applicants; mainly because of the drain on admissions tutors' time. Whether or not you are invited to any will depend on the policy of the languages departments at the institutions you choose. Some are content to rely on the reference on the UCAS form to assess your ability and make offers of places by post. A significant number of admissions tutors in languages departments do however, want to hear you speak or to test your language in other ways – some use written tests – and for this reason if you are applying for a languages course you might be invited to more interviews than friends who are applying for other subjects. Nearly all the institutions that do not interview *do* hold open days when they arrange for you to be shown round a department and meet students and staff. These give you the chance to ask any questions you have, decide whether the course is right for you and of course, to look round the university/college itself and the town or surrounding area.

When you have had decisions from all your institutions you must choose between any offers you have been made. In fairness to other applicants, each person is allowed to hold only two offers; one of which is a firm choice and the other an 'insurance' (usually with less difficult conditions).

Offers of interviews and places can happen *at any time* between your sending in the form and the beginning of May, although the peak time is the early spring term. There is no set timetable. Some institutions handle applications more quickly than others. If you have had no interviews at the point when all your friends have had several this is not necessarily bad news, and it is important not to panic!

Should you be unfortunate enough to receive no offers or not get high enough grades when the exam results come out UCAS operates a Clearing system during August and September. This system is described fully in another book in this series, *Clearing the Way*.

The UCAS form

The entire form is important. It is essential to do practice drafts first so that you can fill in the final version with no crossings out or spelling mistakes. It's also important to obey the rule about using black ink and to write (or type) neatly. This is because the form is going to be photocopied and reduced to about two thirds of its original size. A word of advice about typing though. Don't attempt this, particularly if using a word processor, unless you are sure that you know how to set the margins and tabs properly. Or at least, use a photocopied form to practise on first. Your school may run out of UCAS forms if too many students request extra ones because they have ruined the first one and there could be a delay in obtaining further supplies from UCAS.

A particularly important section and one which applicants often find difficult is Section 10. This is the blank space where you try to sell yourself and convince an admissions tutor that you should be offered a place, by describing your interests, hobbies, and general out-of-school activities in addition to your reasons for choosing the particular course.

Why should admissions tutors want to know all these details ? Isn't getting high exam grades going to be enough? No, not entirely. They want to teach students who are genuinely motivated to do their course. Where language courses are concerned it is particularly important that they know that you have done your research properly. If you are applying for the courses that contain a significant amount of literature, this section should contain information about the authors you read. Alternatively, they want to see your reasons for choosing courses with another emphasis.

Admissions tutors generally like consistency. They know the syllabuses at other institutions and usually regard with suspicion an application that mixes different types of course. 'Has this student really read the prospectus?' they ask. 'Why has s/he applied for two more courses like mine but three which have a totally different content?'

They also want to be sure that you can balance your time and won't be in a constant panic trying to meet deadlines for essays and assignments, so information on how you spend your spare time is helpful. (It provides proof of time management as much as anything ie you have a weekend job or play in a sports team every Saturday, yet still cope with your academic work.)

The general advice to students filling in their forms is to try to give a picture of a balanced all-round person who enjoys academic work but also has time for other things, so any evidence of reading which is not required by the exam syllabus, membership of relevant societies, related work experience and so on is important. It is usual also to put down any school activities in which you participate or positions of responsibility you hold.

Admissions tutors in all subjects also want to see evidence of commitment to their course. You are applying for a language course. The evidence of general interests *is* important. They want students with a wide range of interests snd enquiring minds. So don't omit these. BUT do devote the larger part of this space to explaining why you want to study languages further and what interests and hobbies you have that are relevant. Examples of things to include are:

- the part of the exam syllabus that you enjoy most – and why

- details of a project you have done

- possible future career plans

- a paragraph about any exchanges or study visits you have participated in

61

- information on what newspapers and magazines you read in the foreign language
- the fact that you have a penfriend and correspond regularly with him or her.

All of these points are helping to set up possible interview questions.

If you are applying to learn a new language, give any evidence you can of the fact that you learn quickly – for example, you did A-level Spanish from scratch in two years – or steps you have already taken to learn one outside school.

Combined/joint courses

If you are applying for a combined course, don't neglect to give information on your reasons for choosing the other subject. Your form will be considered by *two* admissions tutors, each of whom is looking for evidence of motivation. So you will have to give equal attention to your interest in business studies, law, music or politics. You will probably run out of space! There is even more reason to do a practice draft several times until you can get it down to size.

Other hints

- Don't put down anything you could not talk about at an interview.

- Do keep a copy of the UCAS form so that you can remember what interests you claimed to have.

- If you really cannot fit all that you want to say into Section 10, you could ask the member of staff writing your reference if they could include some of it in their space. If, for example, they include the fact that you have taken part in exchange visits every year or found yourself a summer job in France on the reference page, the information will still be there for admissions tutors to read, they can still ask you questions on it at interview and you will have more room to write the remainder of what you want to get across in Section 10.

Section 10 in more detail

Admissions tutors' advice

'I look for evidence of awareness of Europe and of things European, its politics and cultural past. Our course is in languages **and** European studies. I also like to see evidence of visits to countries where their proposed language is spoken; and of a general positive attitude to learning languages. Do they seize the opportunity to speak French and German? Have they perhaps taught themselves a little Italian or Spanish if they want to take up one of these? I look for evidence of wide reading, in the foreign language and in English – and in substantial volume. Do they read only articles? Will a novel by Zola therefore prove difficult? Which newspapers do they read? (Reading only tabloids counted against one applicant last year.)

I concentrate on the motivation for the course but I do glance at their out-of-school interests. Like most of my colleagues, I'm not too happy about candidates who appear to spend 24 hours a day working to pass their A-levels.'

**Course tutor, BA in Modern Languages
and European Studies**

'I look for a record of serious language study. They are highly unlikely to have studied mine previously, but if they have learned any modern language in depth they will appreciate what is involved in learning another. If they have done Greek, Russian or any other with a different alphabet – even a little on a self-taught basis – so much the better.'

Course tutor, Oriental Languages

'I look at the track record of language learning. They should have two languages at good grades at GCSE as an absolute minimum and be taking one at A-level. Two A-level languages would be better. Some of the candidates have been to Russia and have even taught themselves a little of the language. I look through Section 10 for evidence of this.'

Course tutor, degree course for beginners in Russian

There is no such thing as a standard perfect Section 10. Nor should the two given here as examples be followed slavishly! They are genuine personal statements – whose writers received offers from all the universities they had applied to.

Elizabeth applied for French and Russian. She is taking A-levels in French, English literature and maths. In the first year of her A-level course she took and passed GCSE Spanish with a grade A.

'For a long time I have particularly enjoyed learning foreign languages. As well as the language itself, I have also had an interest in studying the background and culture of the countries involved and examining various topics from a foreign point of view. In my free time at college I took the opportunity of taking a course in Italian for beginners.

I like to travel and I have had the opportunity to go to France many times. These visits have helped me to enhance my language skills and I look forward to residing in the country during my course.

In my leisure time I have done voluntary work, including some time as assistant leader at a youth club in my town and helping at the local Red Cross Disabled Club. More recently, I helped to organise activities at Junior Citizens '94, an event arranged to increase safety awareness in primary school children. This year I have joined the British Trust for Conservation Volunteers and during the summer I spent a rewarding week improving access for visitors to Chesil Beach.

In my spare time I enjoy swimming, aerobics and writing to penfriends in France and Australia. I regularly attend theatre and cinema productions and like to go out with my friends.

I have enjoyed all aspects of college work and hope to benefit a great deal from university.'

Natalie is doing A-level German, English literature and communication studies.

'I thoroughly enjoy studying German and have benefited greatly from an exchange visit to Waiblingen near Stuttgart, where I

was able to progress in both my spoken German and the learning of German culture. Additional boosts have been a German Industry project in which a group of us had to make a product, sell it and entertain a German guest; and the opportunity to conduct correspondence with a German college using electronic mail, enabling me to learn up to date information.

Having been commended for my work and progress throughout my German course has given me further determination to succeed.

I have also enjoyed my other A-levels, especially as I am interested in the media and current affairs. A period of work experience at the East Kent Gazette gave me the opportunity to make the most of my interest in journalism, giving me both insight into the running of a newspaper and the responsibility of helping the news team. To add to my experience I have become a member of a print journalism group which involves total commitment and input for writing of articles for the college column of the local newspaper. I like to take opportunities as they arise and as part of my college programme I have completed a course in word processing to improve my computer literacy. I take both an active and passive role in the theatre which complements my English studies and enjoyment in reading. I have recently seen Shakespeare's 'A Midsummer Night's Dream' and Dickens' 'Great Expectations'. As well as attending the theatre I have taken great pride in receiving an award for my principal performance in two productions. Amongst the wide range of sports I play, badminton is a particular favourite, both in college and in my spare time playing for a local club.

I like travelling and have visited New Zealand, America and parts of Europe. Ultimately, I have a view to working abroad on a long-term basis.'

☐ NON-UCAS APPLICATIONS

Much of what goes before applies to the way in which you complete other application forms. The length of form and the amount of space it gives you to write about yourself will vary since colleges design their own. They are usually shorter than the UCAS form and have a much smaller section for personal information than the UCAS Section 10. Admissions staff still want to know the same things though ie why you want to do the course; why you want to study the particular language; what you do in your own time to improve your knowledge of it and so on.

The major difference between college forms and the UCAS one is that they are individual. They are not photocopied and distributed centrally. You have to fill in one form for each college you apply to. This does give you scope to write a paragraph about why you want to study at that particular college and in that particular area. (For example, 'I am applying to take this course at X College because I know that it has an excellent reputation both for teaching and for helping its students to find employment when they leave. Former students from my school have taken this course and have recommended it highly.')

The majority of non-UCAS applications will be for bi-lingual secretarial courses. In addition to writing about an interest in languages it is important to include something about career aspirations and to make it clear that you do know what the job of a secretary/personal assistant involves.

Chapter Thirteen
GETTING THE MOST FROM YOUR INTERVIEW

Do you enjoy interviews? Or dread them? Most people would admit to being nervous before them. Admissions tutors know this however, and always make allowances for nerves. You can also do a great deal to make them easier by careful preparation beforehand.

Interviews are actually declining in importance. University and college staff are under pressure with more students to teach. They are hard pressed to offer applicants individual interviews. Candidates and their teachers often complain that they can lose as much as two days of A-level work in travelling half way across the country for a 20 minute interview. Even modern language admissions staff are becoming more willing to rely on subject teachers' assessment of your ability. They then invite all applicants to whom they have offered places to an open day when they can give group talks and show numbers of students round the department. However, many do still like to meet applicants face to face. They also like to hear them speak in the language they have applied to study.

☐ PREPARATION

There is some general advice which applies to all college and university interviews.

You should be ready to answer questions about your present course/syllabus and what you like or dislike about it.

You can make intelligent guesses about other likely questions and rehearse some answers to them. (Don't make these sound too pat and prepared, however.)

Fairly common questions are:

1. Why have you applied for this particular course?

2. What do you know about the way in which it is taught?

3. Why have you applied to do it here?

4. Why have you applied to the other courses you have chosen?

Re-reading the prospectus and any other course information you have before the interview should help you with the answers to 2. and 3. Why not take the prospectus with you and read it on the way to the interview?

Question 4 is often asked and candidates don't always expect it. Remember that in the case of UCAS applications admissions tutors see the list of all the places you have chosen. They normally have a fair idea of how their subject is taught in other institutions and are often interested to see whether you have been consistent in choosing courses with similar approaches.

Examples of questions specific to language courses

You are often expected to:

- discuss the books you are studying

- talk about visits to other countries

- say what you know about current affairs in the country where the language is spoken

- talk about foreign newspapers and magazines you read

- talk in one of your A-level languages.

☐ TIPS FOR THE INTERVIEW

- Get there early. Allow plenty of time.

- Dress comfortably. You are not being interviewed for a job as a lawyer or accountant. Suits are not needed. The interviewer/s probably won't be wearing one. It is best to be smartly casual and not to wear anything that is likely to make you feel uncomfortable or nervous.

- During the interview the golden rule is DON'T BLUFF. If you don't understand a question ask for it to be rephrased or explained.

- You will almost certainly be asked whether you have any questions to ask. Have some ready. Questions on some detailed aspect of the course or on the options are good ones to ask.

Analyse your answers afterwards and work out if you could have answered any questions better. It's all good practice for next time. Don't expect an offer of a place immediately. The decision may take a few days.

☐ THREE STUDENTS DESCRIBE THEIR INTERVIEWS

Student applying for single subject German

'It was with one person, lasted about 20 minutes and was conducted partly in German; partly in English. In German I was asked whether I had been to Germany and then to talk about things I had done there. He also asked questions about my A-level course and what I enjoyed most on it. I mentioned one of the plays we are reading. It contains quite a lot of moral scenes and he asked my opinion of those. He had also noticed from my UCAS form that environmental science was one of my A-levels and asked me about my interest in environmental problems.

When he switched to English the interviewer asked my reasons for choosing German and then asked why I had chosen that university. I was prepared for this and had some answers ready. I said that I had chosen universities within a certain distance of my home town and I also said that I had chosen this particular course because of the options that were offered. I had reread the prospectus the day before the interview and I explained why I thought I would like them.

'I didn't find it difficult. It was very informal. The interviewer was relaxed and made the whole thing more like a discussion. It was made easier by the fact that I had tried to anticipate some of the questions and had made some notes in German for possible answers.'

Student applying for French and Russian

'I was interviewed by a lecturer from the Russian Department, who obviously couldn't interview me in Russian because I am applying for a beginners' course. He began by asking questions about my A-level French course. He wanted to be sure that I enjoyed reading because the degree course will contain some literature, and asked me questions on two texts we are doing, 'Les Mains sales' by Sartre and 'L'Avare' by Molière. Describing the plot of 'Les Mains sales' was OK but I found discussing Sartre's political views a bit tricky.

'Next, he asked about my reasons for wishing to begin Russian. I explained that I liked learning new languages (I have GCSE German and I also did GCSE Spanish in my first A-level year), that I was looking forward to the challenge of learning one with a different alphabet and that I was also interested in the history of Russia. My French lecturer had suggested I stress that I can pick up languages quickly so I also talked about the beginners' Italian course I am doing in my free time and an evening class I am doing in Russian. I had begun it after my UCAS form had gone in, so it had not been mentioned in my reference. He was very interested in that and, I think, impressed.

'He also asked whether I had had the opportunity to visit Russia. Unfortunately, I haven't, so we talked instead about my visits to France.'

Student applying for German

'The letter inviting me to interview told me that part of it would be in German, so I was prepared. The interviewer was very friendly and made me feel relaxed. He started by saying in German that he was going to ask me some questions and that I mustn't worry too much about grammar or getting everything exactly right. He just wanted to hear me speak. We spoke in German for about 15 minutes – about a visit I had made to Germany, the differences between English and German schools and what I thought about the country. He also asked about my out-of-school interests.

'The English part also lasted about 15 minutes. He asked me why I wanted to do German and why I had chosen that *university. I had read recently in a newspaper that it was very highly rated for German and that they were building a new postgraduate centre so I mentioned both of those points. I also said that all my choices were universities which would arrange for me to spend the year abroad as an assistant rather than as a student. He wanted to know how much literature I was doing and he knew the two plays I mentioned, so asked me some questions on character analysis. He also asked which of the four skills, reading, listening, writing and speaking, I found most difficult. I was honest and said 'reading' but he said that was not an impossible problem.*

'It was quite an easy interview, but I had prepared well. My German teacher had given me some hints on possible interview questions and I had reread the prospectus the day before going so I was ready with a few questions of my own to ask.'

Chapter Fourteen
THE ERASMUS PROGRAMME

You might be thumbing through this book, wondering whether to study languages at university or whether to do a different subject. Suppose you would really rather do something else but feel it a shame to drop a language that you have studied up to A-level?

Well, you don't have to make such a clear-cut choice. First of all, have you looked at the chapters on courses to see whether there is a joint course combining a language with your favourite subject? If there isn't one, you might be just the sort of person who would benefit from ERASMUS.

Erasmus was a Dutch renaissance scholar who spoke several languages and studied in Belgium, England, France, Germany, Italy, and Switzerland. His name also forms the acronym for a European Union initiative, the European Action Scheme for the Mobility of University Students. It is designed to help students in the EU and also in European Free Trade Association (EFTA) countries to spend a part of their higher education course in another country.

Institutions link with each other to provide reciprocal hospitality for students. The ERASMUS programme helps with funding and usually gives students a small additional grant to help cover their costs.

Institutions participating in ERASMUS:

- charge no fees to exchange students (who continue to pay them to their home university)

- guarantee academic recognition for the period of study abroad

- provide guest students with all the facilities provided for their own students

- give their own students language tuition before they go abroad.

As an ERASMUS student you would study your *own* subject *at* a European institution *in* the language of the country. In other words you could spend a period abroad whether your subject was history, maths, English, social work or architecture. Your foreign language fluency would improve as would your appreciation of the country's culture – and you would make friends with students of other nationalities. (Probably with several nationalities, because institutions will be acting as hosts to students from many different countries.)

The period of study must be between three and 12 months – but you don't normally get to decide that. The universities and colleges draw up their own programmes: some opt for three months, some for five, others for nine.

You don't have to have an A-level in the language you want to improve. GCSE will often suffice if you are very motivated and in some cases you can be an absolute beginner. The ERASMUS funding pays for institutions to provide intensive language tuition. There have been examples of British chemistry and history students going to Denmark and Greece with no knowledge of the language before beginning intensive tuition, and coping very well with lectures and life in those countries.

How do you find out where ERASMUS schemes are run?

• Universities and colleges say so in their prospectuses.

• Look in *ERASMUS – The UK Guide* published by ISCO Publications which might be in your school or college library. This gives a master list of all the institutions which take part in the programme, shows which subjects are included and the length of the study period.

Chapter Fifteen
FINANCING YOUR STUDY

You have to live for three or four years. Government support to students is becoming less generous each year – and not all courses qualify for support. The main difference is between those which attract a mandatory grant – this means local education authorities are obliged to provide some assistance – and those that do not. The latter category unfortunately includes secretarial courses.

Normally, you will not receive a grant for courses studied at private institutions.

There are booklets that describe the grants and loans systems. The addresses from which you can get them are given in the book list in Chapter Sixteen. What follows is a summary of the main points.

☐ GRANTS

To qualify for a grant you must normally have been resident in Britain for the three years before your course starts. (Exceptions are usually made for people whose parents have been temporarily working abroad.)

In England and Wales, grants are made by Local Education Authorities (LEAs); in Northern Ireland by Education and Library Boards. In Scotland the Scottish Office Education Department deals with mandatory grants while discretionary grants are made by Regional or Islands Councils.

These authorities are not obliged to give grants to students on courses other than those on a list compiled by the Government.

These are known as designated courses and include:
• first degrees
• Diplomas of Higher Education
• Higher National Diplomas
• certain other certificates and diplomas on the designated list.

So if yours is a HND or degree course and it is at a state-funded university or college you should be OK.

☐ NON-DESIGNATED COURSES

Authorities may award 'discretionary grants' for non-designated courses. This means, as the title suggests, that they have the power to decide whether to give you a grant at all. The amount too is at their discretion. They don't even have to pay your fees. Most authorities have their own lists of courses they will support.

The situation regarding bi-lingual secretarial courses is that most authorities do pay the tuition fees and give discretionary grants. However, as they do vary, you will need to check your own authority's policy.

☐ WHAT IS A MANDATORY GRANT SUPPOSED TO COVER?

It's supposed to contribute to your living expenses in *term time*: accommodation, food, books and travel from home to university or college and daily travel there.

It doesn't include your tuition fees. These are paid direct to the university or college on your behalf, so you need not worry about them.

☐ APPLYING FOR A GRANT

You will need to apply to the authority in whose area you are living *on 30 June immediately prior to the commencement of the course*. That authority then pays your fees and grant for the length of the course, even if your parents move to another area during that time.

Most authorities expect you to get application forms from them in the spring term of your last year at school or college. Your careers teacher, head of sixth form, etc can tell you where to write, but you may find that a supply is sent to school/college.

The closing date for mandatory grant applications is, surprisingly, the end of your first term in higher education, and the money can be paid in arrears. But you'll want it before then. You will find that your authority has its own closing date which you must abide by if you want your cheque for the start of term.

Closing dates for discretionary grant applications are decided by each authority and are usually earlier – often in June. It is essential to find out when these are. Authorities have a nasty habit of not accepting late application forms.

☐ WHAT YOU GET

Mandatory grants

The figures change each year because the Government intends to reduce the grant amount each year and increase the amount available as a student loan until a point is reached where the two are roughly equal.

The maximum rates for the academic year 1995/96 were:

Students living away from home and studying:

In London	£2,340
Elsewhere	£1,885

Students living at their parents' home   £1,530

Did you notice the word 'maximum'?

That is because grants are means-tested. How much you get depends on your family's income. The amount is calculated on *residual* income, a figure arrived at by starting with the combined gross income of both your parents and subtracting from that allowances for commitments such as life assurance, pension and mortgage contributions and for other dependants.

Sliding scales are then applied, with parents being expected to make a contribution according to the level of the residual income.

For example:

On a residual income of £15,510 the parental contribution is £45 and your grant cheque is reduced by that amount.

At £20,000 the parental contribution is £409
at £25,000 ....£968
at £30,000 ....£1,550.

Unfortunately, if your parents are unable or unwilling to give you the amount calculated you don't get any more.

Some of your own income is also taken into account. If you receive more than £3,865 from sponsorships or scholarships, your grant will be reduced. You may *earn* as much as you can - but may, of course, have to pay income tax.

Discretionary Grants

Authorities decide how much they can afford to pay in grants each year and then decide how to award them. As everything is at their discretion, it is impossible to try and give any hard-and-fast rules.

However, a fairly common policy is that as far as secretarial courses are concerned, they will pay tuition fees and often give a maintenance grant, even if this is smaller than the amount of a mandatory one.

☐ STUDENT LOANS

Loans are not means-tested. Maximum rates for 1995/96 were as follows.

Students living away from home and studying:

	Full Year	Final Year
In London	£1,695	£1,240
Elsewhere	£1,385	£1,010

	Full Year	Final Year
Students living at their parents' home	£1,065	£780

Special rate

	Full Year	Final Year
Students living at home and receiving the home rate	£1,530	£1,240

(The Special Rate is for students in London, living away from home, whose LEA considers that they could attend the course from their parents home.)

The final year loan figure is smaller because it does not include an amount for the summer vacation.

You can apply for a loan if you are attending one of the courses designated for a mandatory grant and are a full-time student under 50 when the course starts.

Applying

You cannot apply for a loan until you have enrolled on an approved course. The scheme is administered by the *Student Loans Company* which sends supplies of application forms to higher education institutions. The loan is paid directly into your bank account.

Repayments

You will not have to begin repayments until the April after your course finishes. You may take up to five years to repay in 60 instalments or pay it off more quickly if you wish. Anyone whose income is less than 85 per cent of national average earnings may defer payments for a year at a time.

The rate of interest is variable. The Government announces what it will be each year, basing the calculation on the Retail Price Index. As an example, the rate for the year ending 31 August 1995 was 2.3 per cent (the annual inflation rate).

☐ OTHER SOURCES OF FINANCE

Overdrafts

There are other people willing to lend you money, such as banks and building societies who see you as future customers. While you are a student they treat you quite well by waiving bank charges and allowing you interest-free overdrafts up to an agreed figure, usually £300-£400 per year. Their charges are high, though, if you break the rules.

Access Funds

These are sums which individual colleges and universities have to help students in severe financial difficulties. It is up to them to decide how to allocate them and how to define financial hardship.

Career Development Loans

These are available to help people pay for career-related courses which are not eligible for grants. You can borrow up to £8,000 to cover 80 per cent of course fees from certain banks which have an agreement with the Department of Education and Employment. (The Department pays the interest while you are on the course.)

Some people use career development loans to finance training at private secretarial colleges or to pay for intensive language courses in private language schools.

Chapter Sixteen
FURTHER INFORMATION

☐ BOOK LIST

Careers

Careers Using Languages, Helen Steadman, Kogan Page (priced).

Working In Languages, Careers and Occupational Information Centre (COIC) (priced).

Working In Tourism, COIC (priced).

Courses

University and College Entrance, a publication for UCAS by Sheed and Ward (priced publication).

Directory of Higher Education, Hobsons Publishing PLC (priced).

UCAS Handbook (free).

ERASMUS, The UK Guide, from ISCO Publications, 12a-18a Princess Way, Camberley, Surrey GU15 3SP (priced publication) Contains information on courses which include a period of study at linked institutions in European Union countries.

The Complete Degree Course Offers, Brian Heap, Trotman and Co. (priced publication).

How to Choose your HND Course, Eric Whittington, Trotman and Co. (priced publication).

The Potter Guide to Higher Education, Dalebank Books, (priced). Also available on ECCTIS.

CRAC Degree Course Guides (priced), Hobsons Publishing PLC. *The Handbook of Initial Teacher Training in England and Wales*, NATFHE/Linneys (priced publication).

The Guide to Training in Secretarial and Office Skills, Angela Mortimer plc in conjunction with Hobsons Publishing PLC.

Teenager's Vacation Guide to Work, Study and Adventure, Published by Vacation Work (priced publication).

Study Holidays, Central Bureau for International Visits and Exchanges (priced).

Finance

Hard Cash, Alan Jamieson, Hobsons Publishing PLC (priced).

Student Life: A Survival Guide, Natasha Roe, Hobsons Publishing PLC (priced).

Students' Money Matters, Gwenda Thomas, Trotman and Co. (priced publication).

Sponsorship for Students, Hobsons Publishing PLC (priced).

Student Grants and Loans, a free booklet available from:

- Department for Education Publications Centre, PO Box 2193, London E15 2EU
- Scottish Office Education Department, Gyleview House, 3 Redheughs Rigg, South Gyle, Edinburgh EH12 9HH
- Department of Education for Northern Ireland, Rathgael House, Balloo Road, Bangor, County Down, BT19 7PR
- Welsh Office Training, Enterprise and Education Department, 3rd Floor, Companies House, Crown Way, Cardiff CF4 3UT.

Vacation work

A Year Off... a Year On?, Suzanne Straw, Hobsons Publishing PLC (priced).

Working Holidays, Central Bureau for Educational Visits and Exchanges (priced).

Adventure Holidays
Summer Jobs Abroad
Teenagers Vacation Guide

The International Directory of Voluntary Work
Work Your Way Around the World

All by Vacation Work Publications, 9 Park End Street, Oxford
(priced publications).

☐ USEFUL ADDRESSES

UCAS
Fulton House, Jessop Avenue, Cheltenham, Gloucestershire
GL50 3SH. Tel: 01242 227788

The Institute of Linguists
24a Highbury Grove, London N5 2DQ.

The Institute of Translation and Interpreting
377 City Road, London EC1V 1NA. Tel: 0171 713 7600

The Central Bureau for Educational Visits and Exchanges
10 Spring Gardens, London SW1A 2BN. Tel: 0171 389 4004

The Association for Language Learning
16 Regent Place, Rugby, Warwickshire CV21 2PN.

Association of Language Excellence Centres (ALEX)
PO Box 178, Manchester M60 ILL.

Alliance Française
1 Dorset Square, London NW1 6PU. Tel: 0171 723 6439

Institut Français
17 Queensberry Place, London SW7 2DT.

Goethe Institut
50 Prince's Gate, Exhibition Road, London SW7 2PH. Tel: 0171 411
3436/3451

Italian Cultural Institute
39 Belgrave Square, London SW1X 8NX. Tel: 0171 235 1461

Instituto Cervantes (Spanish)
102 Eaton Square, London SW1W 9AN. Tel: 0171 235 1485